TOSEL®
READING SERIES

JUNIOR

READING

1

KB158123

ITC International TOSEL Committee

CONTENTS

About TOSEL®

TOSEL (Test of Skills in the English Language) was developed to meet the demand for a more effective assessment of English as a foreign language for learners from specific cultural settings.

TOSEL evaluates and certifies the proficiency levels of English learners, from the age of 4 through adulthood, along with academic and job performance results.

Background

- Other English tests are ineffective in accurately measuring individual abilities
- Overuse of US-dominated testing systems in diverse cultural and educational contexts in the global English language learning market

Functions & Usage

- Assessment is categorized into 7 levels
- Used as a qualification for academic excellence for school admissions
- Used as a test to assess the English proficiency in the corporate and public sectors

Goals

- Create an effective tool for assessing and evaluating the English skills of English language learners
- Implement efficient and accessible testing systems and methods
- Provide constructive and developmental English education guidance

TOSEL® Strength

LEVELED ASSESSMENTS

An established English test system fit for seven different levels according to learners' cognitive development

ACCURATE DIAGNOSIS

A systematic and scientific diagnosis of learners' English proficiency

EXTENSIVE MATERIALS

Supplementary materials to help learners in an EFL environment to prepare for TOSEL and improve their proficiency

SUFFICIENT DATA

Content for each level developed by using data accumulated from more than 2,000,000 TOSEL test takers delegated at 15,000 schools and academies

CLASSIFIED AREAS OF INTELLIGENCE

Content designed to foster and expand the strengths of each student, categorized by the eight areas of intelligence

CONTINUITY

A complete course of English education ranging from kindergarten, elementary school, middle school, high schoool, and up to adults.

HIGH RELIABILITY

A high reliability level (Cronbach's alpha: .904 for elementary school students / .864 for university students) proven by several studies (Oxford University / Modern Language Journal)

SYSTEMATIC & EFFECTIVE ENGLISH EDUCATION

Accurate diagnosis and extensive materials which provide a step-by-step development in English learning, according to the quality of each learner's ability

TOSEL® Level Chart

Seven Separate Assessments

TOSEL divides the test into seven stages, by considering the test takers' cognitive levels, according to different ages. Unlike other assessments based on only one level, TOSEL includes separate assessments for preschool, elementary school, middle school, high school students, and for adults, which also includes both professionals and college students.

TOSEL's reporting system highlights the strengths and weaknesses of each test taker and suggests areas for further development.

COCOON

Suitable for children aged 4-6 (pre-schoolers)

The first step in the TOSEL system, the test is composed of colorful designs and interesting questions to interest young learners and to put them at ease.

Pre-STARTER

Suitable for children aged 7-8 (1st-2nd grades of elementary school)

Evaluates the ability to comprehend simple vocabulary, conversations, and sentences.

STARTER

Suitable for children aged 9-10 (3rd-4th grades of elementary school)

Evaluates the ability to comprehend short sentences and conversations related to everyday situations or topics.

BASIC

Suitable for children aged 11-12 (5th–6th grades of elementary school)

Evaluates the ability to communicate about personal information, daily activities, future plans, and past experiences in written and spoken language.

JUNIOR

Suitable for middle school students

Evaluates the ability to comprehend short paragraphs, practical texts, and speech covering general topics and to participate in simple daily conversations.

HIGH JUNIOR

Suitable for high school students

Evaluates the ability to use English fluently, accurately, and effectively on a wide range of social and academic subjects, as well as the ability to use sentences with a variety of complex structures.

ADVANCED

Suitable for university students and adults

Evaluates the ability to use practical English required for a job or work environment, as well as the ability to use and understand English at the university level.

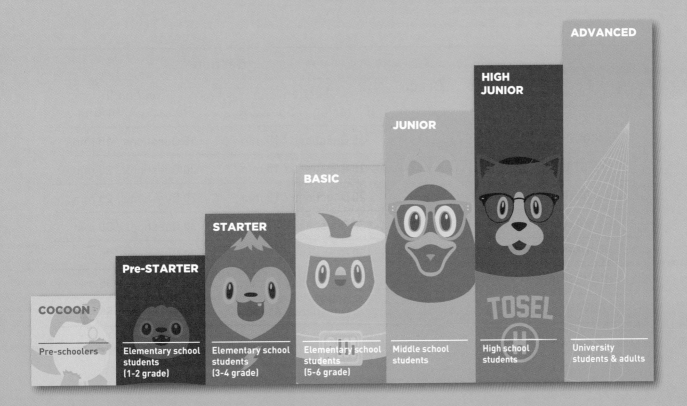

COCOON — Pre-schoolers

Pre-STARTER — Elementary school students (1-2 grade)

STARTER — Elementary school students (3-4 grade)

BASIC — Elementary school students (5-6 grade)

JUNIOR — Middle school students

HIGH JUNIOR — High school students

ADVANCED — University students & adults

Evaluation

Assessing the Four Skills

TOSEL evaluates the four language skills: reading, listening, speaking and writing, through indirect and direct assessment items.

This system of evaluation is part of a concerted effort to break away from materials geared solely toward grammar and reading-oriented education.

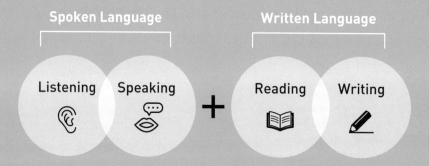

TOSEL Test Information

Level	Score	Grade	Section	
			Section I Listening & Speaking	Section II Reading & Writing
COCOON	100		15 Questions / 15 min	15 Questions / 15 min
Pre-STARTER	100		15 Questions / 15 min	20 Questions / 25 min
STARTER	100		20 Questions / 15 min	20 Questions / 25 min
BASIC	100	1-10	30 Questions / 20 min	30 Questions / 30 min
JUNIOR	100		30 Questions / 20 min	30 Questions / 30 min
HIGH JUNIOR	100		30 Questions / 25 min	35 Questions / 35 min
ADVANCED	990		70 Questions / 45 min	70 Questions / 55 min

Certificates

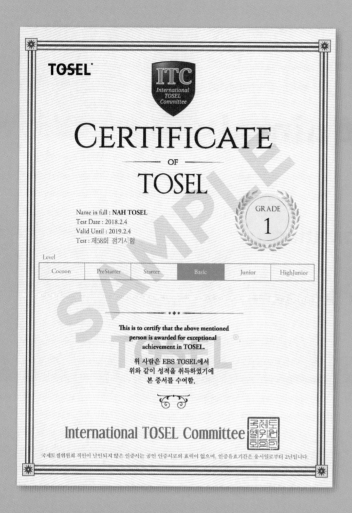

TOSEL Certificate

The International TOSEL Committee officially evaluates and certifies the level of English proficiency of English learners from the age of 4 to adults.

Certified by

Mar. 2010   Korea University
Dec. 2009   The Korean Society of Speech Science
Dec. 2009   The Korea Association of Foreign Language Education
Nov. 2009   The Applied Linguistics Association of Korea
Oct. 2009   The Pan Korea English Teachers Association

CHAPTER 1

Humans and Animals

UNIT 1

Teacher's Book p.44

Animal Communication

Do you think humans and gorillas can have a conversation?

Most animals "speak" a different language from humans. A famous exception was Koko. She was a gorilla who learned American sign language. Koko was born in a zoo, and lived most of her life at a special center. From the age of one, Koko learned sign language from a researcher named Penny Patterson. Patterson also taught Koko to recognize spoken English words. Koko could not use grammar in a sentence. However, she could form the signs for certain words. Using that system, she could ask Patterson and other researchers for things she wanted. According to Patterson, Koko asked for a pet. Therefore, in 1983, the researchers brought Koko some kittens. As a birthday present, she was allowed to keep one of them. She chose a small, gray kitten. He looked like a furry ball, so Koko named him "All Ball." After All Ball died, Koko used sign language to get other pets and to "talk" to humans. During her 46 years, Koko represented communication between humans and animals.

New Words

sign language

n a way of talking using the hands

researcher

n a person who studies something very carefully and scientifically

certain

adj some

according to X

prep X said it

be allowed to do something

v

ex Are you allowed to keep a pet? Then someone said to you, "You can keep that pet."

look like

v

ex If a cloud looks like a fish, the cloud has the shape of a fish.

Part A. Sentence Completion

1.   A: Animals are not _____ to come inside.
     B: But my dog is cold.

   (A)   allow
   (B)   allows
   (C)   allowed
   (D)   allowing

2.   A: I swear that mean-looking monkey talked to me.
     B: Monkeys can't talk, _____?

   (A)   do they
   (B)   can they
   (C)   can't they
   (D)   don't they

Part B. Situational Writing

3.

A cute little _____ is holding a fish in its mouth.

   (A)   koala
   (B)   kitten
   (C)   puppy
   (D)   penguin

4.

I'm learning _____ language from my friend.

   (A)   sign
   (B)   help
   (C)   stop
   (D)   hand

Animals That Could "Speak"

Hoover the Seal	Blackie the Cat	Alex the Parrot	Lucy the Chimp

• Where Maine, USA	• Where Georgia, USA	• Where Illinois, USA	• Where Oklahoma, USA
• When 1971-1985	• When 1980s	• When 1976-2007	• When 1964-1987
Had several children, but they could not talk.	Was trained to say "I love you" and "I want my mama."	Could identify 50 different objects. Knew colors, shapes, and materials.	Knew 250 American Sign Language signs.

5.   What is true about the animals?

(A)   Two were birds.
(B)   None could walk.
(C)   Three lived underwater.
(D)   All four lived in America.

6.   According to the passage, which of the following is NOT true?

(A)   Blackie lived in the 1980s.
(B)   Alex lived to be 31 years old.
(C)   Lucy knew some sign language.
(D)   Hoover taught his children to talk.

Part D. General Reading and Retelling

Most animals "speak" a different language from humans. A famous exception was Koko. She was a gorilla who learned American sign language. Koko was born in a zoo, and lived most of her life at a special center. From the age of one, Koko learned sign language from a researcher named Penny Patterson. Patterson also taught Koko to recognize spoken English words. Koko could not use grammar in a sentence. However, she could form the signs for certain words. Using that system, she could ask Patterson and other researchers for things she wanted. According to Patterson, Koko asked for a pet. Therefore, in 1983, the researchers brought Koko some kittens. As a birthday present, she was allowed to keep one of them. She chose a small, gray kitten. He looked like a furry ball, so Koko named him "All Ball." After All Ball died, Koko used sign language to get other pets and to "talk" to humans. During her 46 years, Koko represented communication between humans and animals.

7. What would be the best title for the passage?

   (A) How Koko Got a Cat
   (B) A Gorilla's Favorite Food
   (C) Why Humans Love Animals
   (D) The Gorilla Who Could "Talk"

8. According to the passage, what is true about Koko?

   (A) She learned to recognize Spanish.
   (B) She learned sign language from Patterson.
   (C) She first used sign language when she was two.
   (D) She could make sentences with proper grammar.

9. According to the passage, what kind of cat did Koko choose?

   (A) a big one
   (B) an ill one
   (C) an old one
   (D) a gray one

10. According to the passage, why did Koko use sign language?

   (A) to get a pet
   (B) to drive a car
   (C) to make a movie
   (D) to go to the jungle

Listening Practice

 Listen and write.

  MP3 J1-1

Animal Communication

Most animals "speak" a different language from humans. A famous exception was Koko. She was a gorilla who learned American ¹ _____ . Koko was born in a zoo, and lived most of her life at a special center. From the age of one, Koko learned sign language from a ² _____ named Penny Patterson. Patterson also taught Koko to recognize spoken English words. Koko could not use grammar in a sentence. However, she could form the signs for ³ _____ words. Using that system, she could ask Patterson and other researchers for things she wanted.

⁴ _____ Patterson, Koko asked for a pet. Therefore, in 1983, the researchers brought Koko some kittens. As a birthday present, she was ⁵ _____ to keep one of them. She chose a small, gray kitten. He ⁶ _____ a furry ball, so Koko named him "All Ball." After All Ball died, Koko used sign language to get other pets and to "talk" to humans. During her 46 years, Koko represented communication between humans and animals.

Word Bank

According to	aloud	sign language
allowed	certain	resercher
sine lenguage	Accordingto	researcher
looked like	serten	look like

 Listen. Pause. Say each sentence.

  MP3 J1-1G

Writing Practice

 Write the words.

1 _____

_n_ a way of talking using the hands

2 _____

_n_ a person who studies something very carefully and scientifically

3 _____

adj some

4 _____ X

prep X said it

5 _____ do something

_v_

ex _____ you _____ keep a pet? Then someone said to you, "You can keep that pet."

6 _____

_v_

ex If a cloud _____s _____ a fish, the cloud has the shape of a fish.

 Write the words in each blank.

Summary

Most animals "speak" a _____ language from humans. However,

a _____ named Koko learned American _____.

Koko symbolized communication between _____ and animals.

Word Puzzle

 Complete the word puzzle.

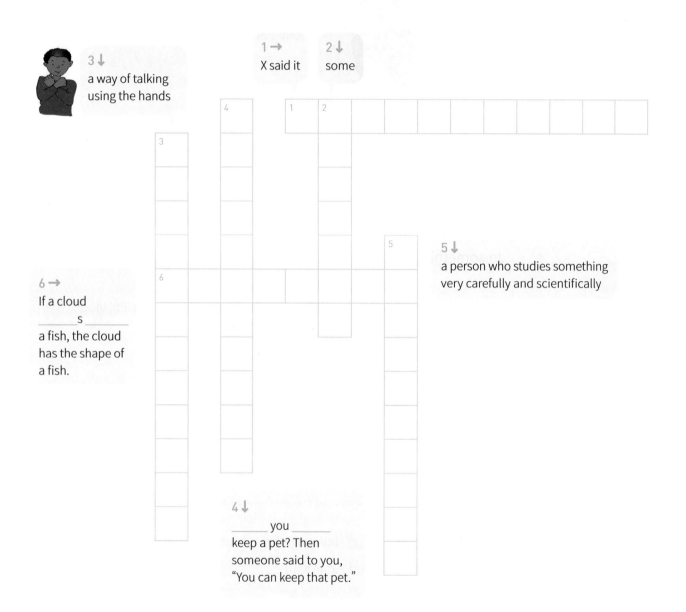

3 ↓ a way of talking using the hands

1 → X said it

2 ↓ some

5 ↓ a person who studies something very carefully and scientifically

6 → If a cloud _____ s _____ a fish, the cloud has the shape of a fish.

4 ↓ _____ you _____ keep a pet? Then someone said to you, "You can keep that pet."

UNIT 2

Teacher's Book
p.48

Animals and Earthquakes

Some animals have special senses.
Can you think of some examples?

UNIT 2 Animals and Earthquakes

Animals may know when earthquakes will happen. Some animals act strangely before there are earthquakes. In 2009, people in Italy noticed many toads leaving their pond. This was not normal. A few days later, there was an earthquake. Scientists believe these events were related. Before an earthquake, chemicals in the earth sometimes mix with water in ponds and lakes. Scientists think that animals who live near them can feel the changes in the water and leave. Animals that live in the ground may also know when an earthquake is coming. In 1975, in China, many people saw snakes coming out of the ground. This was strange because it happened in winter when the snakes were having their winter sleep. One month later, there was an earthquake in the area. Scientists want to learn how this animal behavior is connected to earthquakes. Then perhaps they could guess when there will be an earthquake in the future.

New Words

earthquake

n when the earth shakes suddenly and violently

chemical

n H_2O, CO_2, N_2, ⋯

pond

n an area of water that is smaller than a lake

behavior

n the way that someone or something acts

be connected to

v be linked to

perhaps

adv maybe

Part A. Sentence Completion

1. A: I wanted to see chipmunks, but there are none!
   B: They sleep in their homes _____ winter.

   (A) in
   (B) while
   (C) when
   (D) since

2. A: Did you notice our dog _____ in circles for hours yesterday?
   B: Maybe he sensed something bad.

   (A) runs
   (B) it ran
   (C) to run
   (D) running

Part B. Situational Writing

3.

The animals are resting by a _____.

(A) sink
(B) river
(C) pond
(D) ocean

4.

Be careful when you _____ chemicals in the lab.

(A) mix
(B) burn
(C) drink
(D) wash

Natural disasters, like hurricanes and tornadoes, can happen anytime. That's why it's important to be prepared. To protect your cat or dog, you can prepare an emergency box of supplies.

Emergency kits should include:

1. A good, current photo ID of your cat or dog
2. First aid supplies & guide book
3. 3-day supply of cat or dog food in a waterproof container (be sure to replace food supply to assure it's fresh)
4. Bottled water
5. 2 bowls for pet food and water
6. A safety collar and leash
7. Waste clean-up supplies
8. Medications and medical records (vaccination records)
9. Information of veterinarian and pet care organizations
10. The owner's name, phone, and address

5. According to the passage, what is NOT something that you should have in the emergency box for your pets?

   (A) safety collar and leash
   (B) two bowls of pet food and water
   (C) the contact information of your friend
   (D) a current photo ID of your cat or dog

6. What is a good title for the list?

   (A) How Disasters Affect Our Lives
   (B) Finding Dogs During a Disaster
   (C) Natural Disasters: Family Safety
   (D) Pet Safety: Preparing for Disasters

Part D. General Reading and Retelling

Animals may know when earthquakes will happen. Some animals act strangely before there are earthquakes. In 2009, people in Italy noticed many toads leaving their pond. This was not normal. A few days later, there was an earthquake. Scientists believe these events were related. Before an earthquake, chemicals in the earth sometimes mix with water in ponds and lakes. Scientists think that animals who live near them can feel the changes in the water and leave. Animals that live in the ground may also know when an earthquake is coming. In 1975, in China, many people saw snakes coming out of the ground. This was strange because it happened in winter when the snakes were having their winter sleep. One month later, there was an earthquake in the area. Scientists want to learn how this animal behavior is connected to earthquakes. Then perhaps they could guess when there will be an earthquake in the future.

7. What is the main idea of the passage?

(A) Animals leave their ponds after earthquakes.
(B) Animals may know that earthquakes are coming.
(C) Animals change their shape before an earthquake.
(D) Animals come out of the ground only during earthquakes.

8. According to the passage, what happened in Italy in 2009?

(A) Snakes died underground.
(B) Toads swam deeper into their pond.
(C) Toads went far away from their pond.
(D) Snakes and toads came out of the ground.

9. According to the passage, why was it strange for snakes to come out of the ground in 1975?

(A) They never come out of the ground.
(B) They usually like it when the ground shakes.
(C) They often move around to find other homes.
(D) They usually sleep underground during winter.

10. According to the passage, what might scientists study more closely?

(A) the effects of floods on animals
(B) people's behavior in China and Italy
(C) chemicals in the earth during earthquakes
(D) animal behavior around the time of earthquakes

Listening Practice

 Listen and write.

  MP3 J1-2

Animals and Earthquakes

Animals may know when ¹ _____ will happen. Some animals act strangely before there are earthquakes. In 2009, people in Italy noticed many toads leaving their pond. This was not normal. A few days later, there was an earthquake. Scientists believe these events were related. Before an earthquake, ² _____ in the earth sometimes mix with water in ³ _____ and lakes. Scientists think that animals who live near them can feel the changes in the water and leave. Animals that live in the ground may also know when an earthquake is coming. In 1975, in China, many people saw snakes coming out of the ground. This was strange because it happened in winter when the snakes were having their winter sleep. One month later, there was an earthquake in the area. Scientists want to learn how this animal ⁴ _____ is ⁵ _____ to earthquakes. Then ⁶ _____ they could guess when there will be an earthquake in the future.

Word Bank

perheps	behavior	pondes
earthquakes	earthqakes	connected
perhaps	chemicals	connect
chemical	behevior	ponds

 Listen. Pause. Say each sentence.

  MP3 J1-2G

Writing Practice

 Write the words.

1 _____

n when the earth shakes suddenly and violently

2 _____

n H_2O, CO_2, N_2, ⋯

3 _____

n an area of water that is smaller than a lake

4 _____

n the way that someone or something acts

5 _____

v be linked to

6 _____

adv maybe

 Write the words in each blank.

Summary

Animals may know when _____ will happen. Some animals _____ strangely before earthquakes. Scientists _____ how these animal _____ are related to earthquakes.

Word Puzzle

Complete the word puzzle.

1 →
an area of water that is smaller than a lake

1 ↓
maybe

2 ↓
be linked to

3 →
the way that someone or something acts

4 ↓
when the earth shakes suddenly and violently

5 →
H_2O, CO_2, N_2, ⋯

UNIT 3

Super Babies

Teacher's Book p.53

Did you know that babies have special powers?
What could you do when you were a baby
that you cannot do now?

Babies are amazing. They have superpowers that adults do not have. Here are some of the incredible things that babies can do. First, they are incredibly flexible. Adults have only 206 bones, but babies have around 300 bones in their bodies. As babies grow, their bones connect. Before this, the body of a baby can bend very easily. Babies can even put their feet in their mouths! Another superpower of young babies happens when they are underwater. When babies are put into water, they hold their breath and begin to make swimming movements without even thinking. They lose this ability when they are about six months old. Babies can also swallow and breathe at the same time. When babies swallow, the opening to their lungs is not blocked. Older children and adults find this action impossible, because the inside of their mouth is different from a baby's mouth. These and other baby superpowers are lost as people get older.

New Words

incredible *adj* amazing	**incredibly** *adv* amazingly / extremely
flexible *adj* bending easily	**swallow** *v* **ex** When you <u>swallow</u>, food is pushed down your mouth.
hold your breath *v* **ex** If you <u>hold your breath</u>, you make yourself stop breathing.	**lungs** *n* a pair of breathing organs

Part A. Sentence Completion

1. A: How long can you hold _____ breath underwater?
   B: I don't know. Maybe two minutes.

   (A) its
   (B) your
   (C) one's
   (D) these

2. A: Interesting fact: adults have _____ bones than babies.
   B: What? Are babies a different species?

   (A) few
   (B) little
   (C) least
   (D) fewer

Part B. Situational Writing

3.

This silly alligator is trying to _____ the sun!

(A) lighten
(B) step on
(C) swallow
(D) lay down

4.

_____ your front knee like this and stretch your arms in the air.

(A) Lift
(B) Hug
(C) Bend
(D) Straighten

Superpowers

Nak-Nak is a baby in the Bonn family of superhumans. The Bonns appear in a comic book called 'The Awesomes.' In this comic, Nak-Nak has more powers than any of the other Bonn family members. He uses the following 5 superpowers different amounts of times in the comic:

Shape Changing	= 26 times
Long Jumping	= 14 times
Powerful Hearing	= 10 times
Wall Crawling	= 6 times
Self-copying	= 4 times

5. What is the name of the comic that Nak-Nak appears in?

(A) The Tubulars
(B) The Fantastics
(C) The Awesomes
(D) The Phenomenals

6. Nak-Nak uses his superpowers 60 times in the comic. Which superpower does he use 10% of the time?

(A) Self-copying
(B) Long Jumping
(C) Wall Crawling
(D) Powerful Hearing

Part D. General Reading and Retelling

Babies are amazing. They have superpowers that adults do not have. Here are some of the incredible things that babies can do. First, they are incredibly flexible. Adults have only 206 bones, but babies have around 300 bones in their bodies. As babies grow, their bones connect. Before this, the body of a baby can bend very easily. Babies can even put their feet in their mouths! Another superpower of young babies happens when they are underwater. When babies are put into water, they hold their breath and begin to make swimming movements without even thinking. They lose this ability when they are about six months old. Babies can also swallow and breathe at the same time. When babies swallow, the opening to their lungs is not blocked. Older children and adults find this action impossible, because the inside of their mouth is different from a baby's mouth. These and other baby superpowers are lost as people get older.

7. What is the best title for this passage?

(A) Babies Can Swim
(B) Babies Are Beautiful
(C) Babies Grow Quickly
(D) Babies Have Superpowers

8. How many bones do babies have in their bodies?

(A) 206
(B) 270
(C) 300
(D) 360

9. Why can babies breathe and swallow at the same time?

(A) They have learned how to do it.
(B) They have a special inner mouth shape.
(C) They do not need as much oxygen as adults.
(D) They were swimming in their mother's bellies.

10. What is probably the main reason that babies can easily put their feet in their mouths?

(A) Their feet are clean.
(B) Their ankles are strong.
(C) Their bodies can bend easily.
(D) They do not walk on their feet.

Listening Practice

 Listen and write.

  MP3 J1-3

Super Babies

Babies are amazing. They have superpowers that adults do not have. Here are some of the ¹_____ things that babies can do. First, they are ²_____ ³_____. Adults have only 206 bones, but babies have around 300 bones in their bodies. As babies grow, their bones connect. Before this, the body of a baby can bend very easily. Babies can even put their feet in their mouths! Another superpower of young babies happens when they are underwater. When babies are put into water, they ⁴_____ and begin to make swimming movements without even thinking. They lose this ability when they are about six months old. Babies can also ⁵_____ and breathe at the same time. When babies swallow, the opening to their ⁶_____ is not blocked. Older children and adults find this action impossible, because the inside of their mouth is different from a baby's mouth. These and other baby superpowers are lost as people get older.

Word Bank

flexble	incredible	flexible
swalow	incredibly	swallow
incredeble	lungs	holder breath
hold their breath	incredebly	langs

 Listen. Pause. Say each sentence.

  MP3 J1-3G

Writing Practice

Write the words.

1 _____

adj amazing

2 _____

adv amazingly / extremely

3 _____

adj bending easily

4 _____

v

ex When you _____, food is pushed down your mouth.

5 _____

v

ex If you _____, you make yourself stop breathing.

6 _____

n a pair of breathing organs

Write the words in each blank.

Summary

Babies can do _____ things. They are very _____ and can hold their _____ underwater. They can also swallow and breathe at the same time. As babies grow, they lose these and other _____.

Word Puzzle

Complete the word puzzle.

1 ↓
If you _____ , you make yourself stop breathing.

2 →
a pair of breathing organs

3 ↓
bending easily

4 ↓
When you _____ , food is pushed down your mouth.

6 ↓
amazingly / extremely

5 →
amazing

UNIT 4

Teacher's Book
p.57

Pigeons

Are pigeons common where you live?
What do you think of them?

Humans have a strange relationship with pigeons. In many cities around the world, residents dislike these birds. They say that pigeons are ugly or messy. It is true that pigeons can be messy. However, they have a long, interesting link to humans. For example, pigeons were the first birds that humans made pets. Tame pigeons are seen in drawings from 5,000 years ago. Moreover, pigeons have been key to human communication. Long before we had the internet, we used messenger pigeons to deliver notes. Pigeons were crucial for messages during wartime, for example. And even in modern times, messages from a pigeon once reached people more quickly than the internet! Finally, pigeons know who humans are. They can recognize human faces and can even see differences in art by different painters. In short, even if pigeons are messy sometimes, they are still important birds in the history of humans.

New Words

pigeon

n   a bird that commonly lives in cities

resident

n

ex   The people who live in a place are that place's <u>residents</u>.

tame

adj   not wild

key to

adj

ex   If X is <u>key to</u> Y, X is important to Y.

crucial

adj   very important

in short

adv   all in all

Part A. Sentence Completion

1. A: I don't like these pigeons in the street.
    B: I don't _____. They are really dirty.

    (A) also
    (B) either
    (C) same
    (D) neither

2. A: I don't like to exercise. It is boring.
    B: _____ it is a bit boring sometimes, exercise is great for you.

    (A) But
    (B) In spite
    (C) Even if
    (D) Despite

Part B. Situational Writing

3.

He did a _____ of a large pigeon.

    (A) statue
    (B) painting
    (C) ceramic
    (D) message

4.

Your room is very _____.

    (A) white
    (B) clean
    (C) empty
    (D) messy

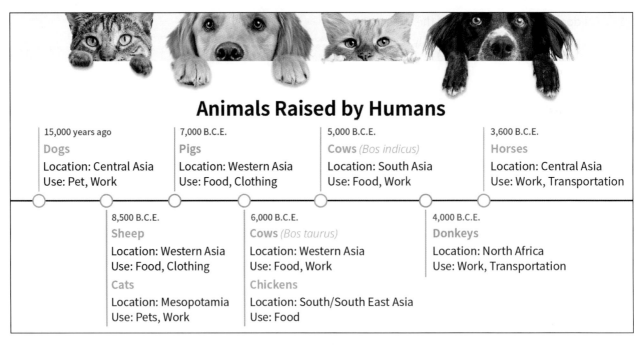

Animals Raised by Humans

15,000 years ago	7,000 B.C.E.	5,000 B.C.E.	3,600 B.C.E.
Dogs	Pigs	Cows (*Bos indicus*)	Horses
Location: Central Asia	Location: Western Asia	Location: South Asia	Location: Central Asia
Use: Pet, Work	Use: Food, Clothing	Use: Food, Work	Use: Work, Transportation

8,500 B.C.E.	6,000 B.C.E.	4,000 B.C.E.
Sheep	Cows (*Bos taurus*)	Donkeys
Location: Western Asia	Location: Western Asia	Location: North Africa
Use: Food, Clothing	Use: Food, Work	Use: Work, Transportation
Cats	Chickens	
Location: Mesopotamia	Location: South/South East Asia	
Use: Pets, Work	Use: Food	

5. Out of the animals in this timeline, what was the most used for?

   (A) food
   (B) work
   (C) clothing
   (D) transportation

6. Which of the following statements is true?

   (A) Cows were only ever used as a food source.
   (B) Horses were used by humans before donkeys.
   (C) Humans raised pigs long before they raised cats.
   (D) Chickens have been used as food for over 8,000 years.

Part D. General Reading and Retelling

Humans have a strange relationship with pigeons. In many cities around the world, residents dislike these birds. They say that pigeons are ugly or messy. It is true that pigeons can be messy. However, they have a long, interesting link to humans. For example, pigeons were the first birds that humans made pets. Tame pigeons are seen in drawings from 5,000 years ago. Moreover, pigeons have been key to human communication. Long before we had the internet, we used messenger pigeons to deliver notes. Pigeons were crucial for messages during wartime, for example. And even in modern times, messages from a pigeon once reached people more quickly than the internet! Finally, pigeons know who humans are. They can recognize human faces and can even see differences in art by different painters. In short, even if pigeons are messy sometimes, they are still important birds in the history of humans.

7. What is the passage mainly about?

   (A) the cost of raising birds as pets
   (B) the most popular birds in the world
   (C) the link between humans and pigeons
   (D) the reason most humans dislike pigeons

8. According to the passage, where are pigeons seen?

   (A) in golden cages
   (B) on top of buildings
   (C) in ancient drawings
   (D) on historical statues

9. According to the passage, what is true?

   (A) Pigeons can read human writing.
   (B) A pigeon drew a picture of a person.
   (C) Most residents in cities love pigeons as pets.
   (D) A pigeon delivered a message faster than the internet.

10. Which is NOT mentioned as a pigeon skill?

   (A) seeing differences in art
   (B) recognizing human faces
   (C) delivering messages during wars
   (D) dropping military weapons on humans

Listen and write.

  MP3 J1-4

Pigeons

Humans have a strange relationship with ¹_____. In many cities around the world, ²_____ dislike these birds. They say that pigeons are ugly or messy. It is true that pigeons can be messy. However, they have a long, interesting link to humans. For example, pigeons were the first birds that humans made pets. ³_____ pigeons are seen in drawings from 5,000 years ago. Moreover, pigeons have been ⁴_____ human communication. Long before we had the internet, we used messenger pigeons to deliver notes. Pigeons were ⁵_____ for messages during wartime, for example. And even in modern times, messages from a pigeon once reached people more quickly than the internet! Finally, pigeons know who humans are. They can recognize human faces and can even see differences in art by different painters. ⁶_____, even if pigeons are messy sometimes, they are still important birds in the history of humans.

Word Bank

crutial	residents	keyto
pigeons	residence	In shot
crucial	pigeon	Tame
Tam	In short	key to

 Listen. Pause. Say each sentence.

  MP3 J1-4G

Writing Practice

  Write the words.

1 _____

n a bird that commonly lives in cities

2 _____

n

ex The people who live in a place are that place's _____s.

3 _____

adj not wild

4 _____

adj

ex If X is _____ Y, X is important to Y.

5 _____

adj very important

6 _____

adv all in all

  Write the words in each blank.

Summary

Although many people _____ them, pigeons have a long _____ with humans. They have helped in _____ and in communication. They are also intelligent. _____, even if pigeons are messy sometimes, they are still important.

Word Puzzle

 Complete the word puzzle.

1 ↓
a bird that commonly lives in cities

2 →
very important

3 ↓
all in all

4 →
The people who live in a place are that place's _____ s.

6 →
If X is _____ Y, X is important to Y.

5 ↓
not wild

Shrek the Sheep

Teacher's Book
p.62

For many years, one sheep from the Bendigo Sheep Station in New Zealand lived just like all the other sheep. He ate on the farm. He slept on the farm. He got his wool shorn (got a haircut) every single year. This is normal for Merino sheep, which have very heavy wool coats.

However, one day this sheep decided he was not going to get a haircut. Instead, he escaped from the farm. Then he hid in caves in the mountains. Somehow, he managed to avoid being caught for six long years. By the time he was caught, his wool was so big he looked like a monster. People started calling him "Shrek the Sheep," after Shrek, a cartoon movie monster.

Shrek's owners finally gave him a haircut. Normally, when a Merino sheep is shorn, there are about 4.5 kilograms of wool. With Shrek, there were 27 kilograms of wool! This would be enough wool to make twenty men's suits.

Shrek became a hero of New Zealand. He even met the leader of the country. Shrek the Sheep died at the age of sixteen. However, his name lives on in New Zealand sheep history.

CHAPTER 2

Math

UNIT 5

The Fields Medal

Teacher's Book p.63

Which prize would you be proudest to win?

UNIT 5 The Fields Medal

Athletes may work towards an Olympic medal. Politicians often want to receive the Nobel Prize. Mathematicians, on the other hand, may hope to receive the Fields Medal. The Fields Medal was named after the Canadian mathematician John Charles Fields. It was first awarded in 1936 to one winner. Since 1950, the medal has been given out every four years. These days, there can be up to four winners at one time. A total of sixty people have won this important award. To get a Fields Medal, a mathematician needs to do some exciting research in mathematics. The winner must also be younger than 40 years old on January 1st that year. Also, Fields Medals are not just for the honor. Medalists also each receive $15,000 in prize money and a gold medal. On the medal is the face of Archimedes, the ancient Greek mathematician. Some people criticize the Fields Medal because older mathematicians cannot receive it. However, this medal is still a big honor in the world of mathematics.

New Words

athlete

n a sports player

medal

n a round prize given to a winner

mathematician

n a person who studies math as a job

ancient

adj really, really, really old

criticize

v say words against something

big honor

n something that makes you feel really proud

Part A. Sentence Completion

1. A: It is a huge _____ to meet you in person.
    B: I feel the same way. I am a big fan of your work!

    (A) honor
    (B) honors
    (C) honored
    (D) honoring

2. A: Who won the Fields Medals this time?
    B: One of the medals was _____ to a German mathematician.

    (A) give
    (B) given
    (C) giving
    (D) to give

Part B. Situational Writing

3.

The winner is wearing a _____ around her neck.

    (A) tie
    (B) scarf
    (C) medal
    (D) trophy

4.

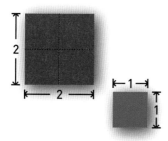

_____ four blue squares can fit in one big red square.

    (A) Up to
    (B) At least
    (C) More than
    (D) Not as many as

Interesting Awards

Award Name	How to Win the Award	Prize
Stinky Shoe Award	Be a child between 5-15 years with extremely smelly running shoes.	$US 2,500
Golden Raspberry Award	Make the worst movies.	A statue of a raspberry painted gold.
The Lanterne Rouge Award	Finish last in the Tour de France bicycle race that goes across France.	A title. Also, sometimes winning the award leads to advertising contracts.

5. Which award celebrates footwear with bad odors?

   (A) The Stinky Shoe
   (B) The Golden Raspberry
   (C) The Lanterne Rouge
   (D) all of them

6. Who would most likely get the Golden Raspberry Award?

   (A) the director of a terrible film
   (B) a 10-year-old Hollywood star
   (C) a cyclist in a French bicycle race
   (D) the winner of the Tour de France

Part D. General Reading and Retelling

Athletes may work towards an Olympic medal. Politicians often want to receive the Nobel Prize. Mathematicians, on the other hand, may hope to receive the Fields Medal. The Fields Medal was named after the Canadian mathematician John Charles Fields. It was first awarded in 1936 to one winner. Since 1950, the medal has been given out every four years. These days, there can be up to four winners at one time. A total of sixty people have won this important award. To get a Fields Medal, a mathematician needs to do some exciting research in mathematics. The winner must also be younger than 40 years old on January 1st that year. Also, Fields Medals are not just for the honor. Medalists also each receive $15,000 in prize money and a gold medal. On the medal is the face of Archimedes, the ancient Greek mathematician. Some people criticize the Fields Medal because older mathematicians cannot receive it. However, this medal is still a big honor in the world of mathematics.

7. What is the main idea of the passage?

    (A) Most athletes hope to win a Fields Medal.
    (B) Many politicians have won the Nobel Prize.
    (C) The Nobel Prize is older than the Olympics.
    (D) The Fields Medal is a big honor for mathematicians.

8. How did the Fields Medal get its name?

    (A) from a company
    (B) from a famous soccer player
    (C) from a Canadian mathematician
    (D) from a large area of grass in Canada

9. What is true about the Fields Medal?

    (A) It is given every four years.
    (B) Winners must be over forty years old.
    (C) There can be fourteen winners each time.
    (D) The first one was given in ancient Greece.

10. Who would most likely win a Fields Medal?

    (A) someone who wrote a hit song
    (B) someone who cured a disease
    (C) someone who invented an electrical device
    (D) someone who solved a hard number problem

Listening Practice

MP3 J1-5

Listen and write.

The Fields Medal

[1] _____ may work towards an Olympic medal. Politicians often want to receive the Nobel Prize. Mathematicians, on the other hand, may hope to receive the Fields Medal. The Fields Medal was named after the Canadian [2] _____ John Charles Fields. It was first awarded in 1936 to one winner. Since 1950, the [3] _____ has been given out every four years. These days, there can be up to four winners at one time. A total of sixty people have won this important award. To get a Fields Medal, a mathematician needs to do some exciting research in mathematics. The winner must also be younger than 40 years old on January 1st that year. Also, Fields Medals are not just for the honor. Medalists also each receive $15,000 in prize money and a gold medal. On the medal is the face of Archimedes, the [4] _____ Greek mathematician. Some people [5] _____ the Fields Medal because older mathematicians cannot receive it. However, this medal is still a big [6] _____ in the world of mathematics.

Word Bank

mathematician	Athletes	mathmatician
criticizes	criticize	ancient
honor	athletes	eincient
metal	onner	medal

Listen. Pause. Say each sentence.

MP3 J1-5G

Writing Practice

 Write the words.

1 _____

n a sports player

2 _____

n a round prize given to a winner

3 _____

n a person who studies math as a job

4 _____

adj really, really, really old

5 _____

v say words against something

6 _____

n something that makes you feel really proud

 Write the words in each blank.

Summary

The Fields Medal is for _____ who did some interesting

_____. Although criticized by some because it is only given to people under

_____, the Fields Medal is still a big _____ for

mathematicians.

Word Puzzle

Complete the word puzzle.

1 ↓
a person who studies math as a job

1 →
a round prize given to a winner

2 ↓
a sports player

4 ↓
say words against something

5 →
something that makes you feel really proud

3 ↓
really, really, really old

UNIT 6

Statistics

Teacher's Book
p.67

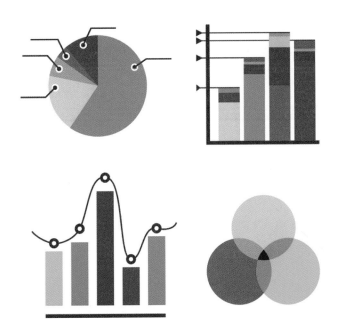

Are you interested in reading charts and graphs?
If so, about what? If not, why not?

Statistics are very useful in our lives. Predicting future weather is one way we use statistics daily. The TV reporters use information in weather models to make predictions. These weather models are computer programs that are built using statistics. A second use of statistics is for our health. Statistics about diseases are in the news a lot. With statistics we can have a better idea of how a disease may hurt us. For example, studies show that 95 percent of lung cancer is linked to smoking. This statistic tells us that there is a good chance of avoiding lung cancer if we don't smoke. Finally, professional sports teams use data to make decisions on playing strategies and finding new players. Sports media also use statistics to make sure sports fans are happy with their team. The weather, diseases, and sports are three areas where statistics are useful in our lives.

New Words

statistic	make predictions
n a piece of math information	*v* say what the future will be
disease	cancer
n an illness	*n* a type of disease in which body cells grow too fast
strategy	make sure
n a plan for doing something	*v* be certain

Part A. Sentence Completion

1. A: Do you think our team will win in the final match?

   B: _____ who will win is not that simple.

   (A) Predict
   (B) Predicted
   (C) Prediction
   (D) Predicting

2. A: Why did you bring an umbrella?

   B: There _____ a good chance of rain later today.

   (A) is
   (B) are
   (C) were
   (D) could

Part B. Situational Writing

3.

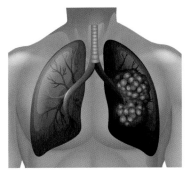

The scientists are looking for a cure for _____.

   (A) lung cancer
   (B) brain tumors
   (C) foot problems
   (D) mouth disease

4.

The presenter showed some _____.

   (A) travel photos
   (B) poetry books
   (C) comedy films
   (D) statistics charts

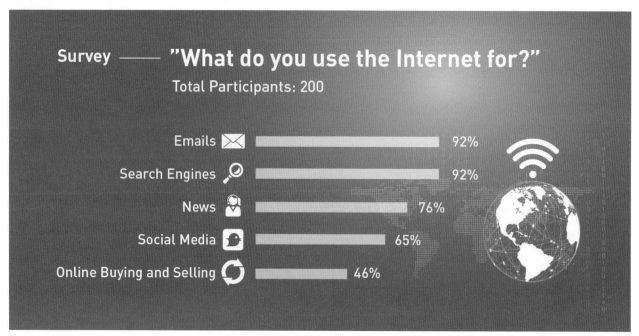

Survey —— "What do you use the Internet for?"
Total Participants: 200

Activity	Percentage
Emails	92%
Search Engines	92%
News	76%
Social Media	65%
Online Buying and Selling	46%

5. According to the survey, what is the internet used for the second least frequently?

(A) News
(B) E-mails
(C) Buy and Sell
(D) Social Media

6. Which internet activity did exactly 92 participants say they do?

(A) sending e-mails
(B) searching the web
(C) reading news articles
(D) buying and selling online

Part D. General Reading and Retelling

Statistics are very useful in our lives. Predicting future weather is one way we use statistics daily. The TV reporters use information in weather models to make predictions. These weather models are computer programs that are built using statistics. A second use of statistics is for our health. Statistics about diseases are in the news a lot. With statistics we can have a better idea of how a disease may hurt us. For example, studies show that 95 percent of lung cancer is linked to smoking. This statistic tells us that there is a good chance of avoiding lung cancer if we don't smoke. Finally, professional sports teams use data to make decisions on playing strategies and finding new players. Sports media also use statistics to make sure sports fans are happy with their team. The weather, diseases, and sports are three areas where statistics are useful in our lives.

7. What would be a good title for this passage?

(A) Statistics in History
(B) Beginner's Statistics
(C) The Power of Statistics
(D) New Discoveries in Statistics

8. What do modern weather reports use to make predictions about the weather?

(A) sky charts
(B) farming calendars
(C) computer programs
(D) encyclopedia articles

9. Which of the following is NOT mentioned as a way that statistics are used in our daily lives?

(A) sports
(B) cooking
(C) weather
(D) diseases

10. Where are you most likely to find this passage?

(A) a textbook
(B) a sports news website
(C) a brochure for a high school
(D) a no-smoking advertisement

Listening Practice

 Listen and write.

  MP3 J1-6

Statistics

Statistics are very useful in our lives. Predicting future weather is one way we use

¹ _____ daily. The TV reporters use information in weather models to

make ² _____ . These weather models are computer programs that are

built using statistics. A second use of statistics is for our health. Statistics about

³ _____ are in the news a lot. With statistics we can have a better idea

of how a disease may hurt us. For example, studies show that 95 percent of lung

⁴ _____ is linked to smoking. This statistic tells us that there is a good

chance of avoiding lung cancer if we don't smoke. Finally, professional sports teams use

data to make decisions on playing ⁵ _____ and finding new players. Sports

media also use statistics to ⁶ _____ sports fans are happy with their team.

The weather, diseases, and sports are three areas where statistics are useful in our lives.

Word Bank

predictions	diseases	prediction
canser	makesure	strategyes
disease	strategies	cancer
statistic	statistics	make sure

 Listen. Pause. Say each sentence.

  MP3 J1-6G

Writing Practice

 Write the words.

1 _____

n   a piece of math information

2 _____

v   say what the future will be

3 _____

n   an illness

4 _____

n   a type of disease in which body cells grow too fast

5 _____

n   a plan for doing something

6 _____

v   be certain

 Write the words in each blank.

Summary

The power of _____ in our lives is very strong. The _____,

_____, and _____ are three areas where statistics are

_____ in our lives.

Word Puzzle

Complete the word puzzle.

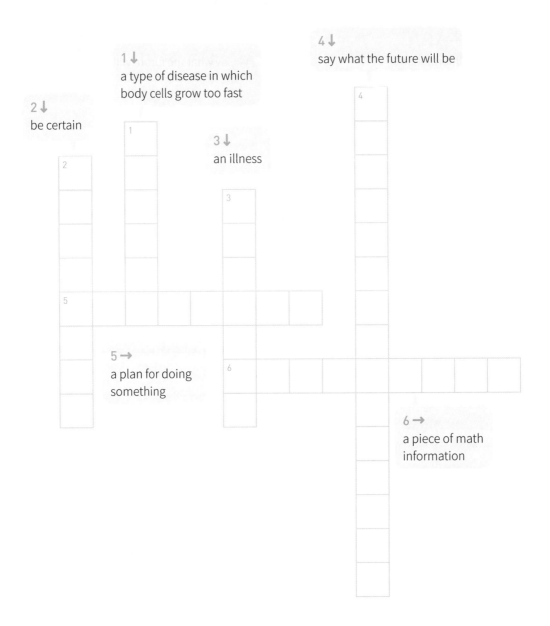

1 ↓
a type of disease in which body cells grow too fast

2 ↓
be certain

3 ↓
an illness

4 ↓
say what the future will be

5 →
a plan for doing something

6 →
a piece of math information

UNIT 7

The Golden Ratio

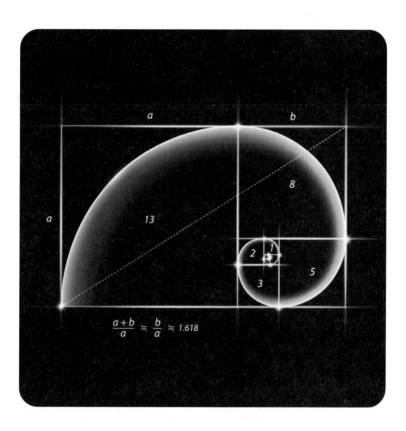

Do you know what this shape is?
Does it remind you of anything?

The Golden Ratio

The Golden Ratio is a special number found in many surprising places. It equals approximately 1.618, but it actually goes on forever without repeating any pattern. Instead of writing it out all the time, mathematicians use the Greek letter Phi (φ) when they write equations. But it is not only mathematicians who have used the Golden Ratio. It has also been used by famous architects and artists. We would not have ancient wonders like the Great Egyptian Pyramids and the Greek Parthenon without this ratio. Da Vinci, Michelangelo, Rembrandt, and Dali all used the Golden Ratio in their artwork as well. These artists felt that if the size of their art followed the Golden Ratio it would be more beautiful. Even nature uses this special number. For example, you can find the Golden Ratio in the spirals of shells, hurricanes, and the Milky Way. Calculating and using the Golden Ratio lets us create beauty and understand the universe we live in.

New Words

ratio

n

The ratio of apples to oranges is 3:2.

equal

v be the same as

The number of apples equals the number of lemons.

approximately

adv around

hurricane

n a storm with a very strong wind

spiral

n a shape like a seashell

calculate

v to use numbers to make another number

Part A. Sentence Completion

1. A: This painting looks perfect, _____ it?
   B: Yeah, the artist worked on it for months.

   (A) don't
   (B) can't
   (C) doesn't
   (D) couldn't

2. A: How should I multiply these numbers?
   B: _____ a calculator might be the easiest way.

   (A) Use
   (B) Using
   (C) If use
   (D) If using

Part B. Situational Writing

3.

This shell has a _____ shape.

   (A) line
   (B) spiral
   (C) square
   (D) rectangular

4.

Jenna wants to be a successful _____.

   (A) architect
   (B) zoologist
   (C) fire fighter
   (D) eye doctor

UNIT 7 The Golden Ratio

The Fibonacci Sequence is one mathematical idea related to the Golden Ratio.
• **Fibonacci Sequence: 1, 1, 2, 3, 5, 8, ...**

To find a number in the Fibonacci Sequence, you add the two numbers before it.

$0+1=1$ → $1+1=2$ → $1+2=3$ → $2+3=5$ → $3+5=8$ → ...

If you keep putting together squares that use Fibonacci Numbers as sides, you get a rectangle that has the Golden Ratio.
Simply begin by adding two _____ [A] _____ of the same size to form a new rectangle. Then keep adding more—each time their length is the same as the longest side of the rectangle.

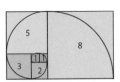

5. What is the next number in the Fibonacci Sequence after 8?

(A) 5
(B) 8
(C) 11
(D) 13

6. What word should go in blank [A]?

(A) lines
(B) squares
(C) triangles
(D) rectangles

Part D. General Reading and Retelling

The Golden Ratio is a special number found in many surprising places. It equals approximately 1.618, but it actually goes on forever without repeating any pattern. Instead of writing it out all the time, mathematicians use the Greek letter Phi (φ) when they write equations. But it is not only mathematicians who have used the Golden Ratio. It has also been used by famous architects and artists. We would not have ancient wonders like the Great Egyptian Pyramids and the Greek Parthenon without this ratio. Da Vinci, Michelangelo, Rembrandt, and Dali all used the Golden Ratio in their artwork as well. These artists felt that if the size of their art followed the Golden Ratio it would be more beautiful. Even nature uses this special number. For example, you can find the Golden Ratio in the spirals of shells, hurricanes, and the Milky Way. Calculating and using the Golden Ratio lets us create beauty and understand the universe we live in.

7. What is the main idea of this passage?

   (A) Artists should start using the Golden Ratio more.
   (B) Ancient architects did not need math to build things.
   (C) The Golden Ratio is seen in both nature and man-made things.
   (D) Mathematicians are searching for a pattern in the Golden Ratio.

8. Which is NOT mentioned as a field that has used the Golden Ratio?

   (A) Art
   (B) Math
   (C) Medicine
   (D) Architecture

9. According to the passage, what shape in nature commonly uses the Golden Ratio?

   (A) circles
   (B) spirals
   (C) triangles
   (D) diamonds

10. According to the passage, which of the following statements is true?

   (A) The Milky Way is a giant golden hurricane.
   (B) Rembrandt was a world-famous gold architect.
   (C) The Golden Ratio has no pattern in its numbers.
   (D) Egyptians learned the Golden Ratio from the Greeks.

Listening Practice

 Listen and write.

  MP3 J1-7

The Golden Ratio

The Golden Ratio is a special number found in many surprising places. It

__1_____ __2_____ 1.618, but it actually goes on forever without

repeating any pattern. Instead of writing it out all the time, mathematicians use the

Greek letter Phi (φ) when they write equations. But it is not only mathematicians who

have used the Golden Ratio. It has also been used by famous architects and artists.

We would not have ancient wonders like the Great Egyptian Pyramids and the Greek

Parthenon without this _3_____. Da Vinci, Michelangelo, Rembrandt, and

Dali all used the Golden Ratio in their artwork as well. These artists felt that if the size

of their art followed the Golden Ratio it would be more beautiful. Even nature uses this

special number. For example, you can find the Golden Ratio in the _4_____

of shells, _5_____, and the Milky Way. _6_____ and using the

Golden Ratio lets us create beauty and understand the universe we live in.

Word Bank

Calculate	approximately	Calculating
ratios	huricanes	spirals
spirels	hurricanes	eqals
ratio	equals	approximate

 Listen. Pause. Say each sentence.

  MP3 J1-7G

Writing Practice

 Write the words.

1 _____

n

The _____ of apples to oranges is 3:2.

2 _____

v be the same as

The number of apples _____s the number of lemons.

3 _____

adv around

4 _____

n a storm with a very strong wind

5 _____

n a shape like a seashell

6 _____

v to use numbers to make another number

 Write the words in each blank.

Summary

The Golden _____ is a special number found in many surprising places.

Mathematicians, architects, and artists have used it. Even _____ uses this

special _____. We can create beauty and understand the

_____ with the Golden Ratio.

Word Puzzle

 Complete the word puzzle.

2 ↓
around

1 →
a shape like a seashell

3 ↓
a storm with a very strong wind

4 ↓
The _____ of apples to oranges is 3:2.

6 ↓
be the same as

The number of apples _____s the number of lemons.

5 →
to use numbers to make another number

UNIT 8

Teacher's Book
p.76

Barcodes

Where can you see barcodes in your daily life?
Do you know how they work?

In a supermarket, you can see many black and white barcodes. The barcodes connect to something called a "Universal Product Code." The first number in the code says what kind of product it is. For example, a "3" means that it is a beauty product. The 2nd to 6th digits show information about the product maker. The 7th to 11th numbers are about the store. And very importantly, each bar code has a "check digit." It is the 12th number in a bar code. The check digit is to see that the other numbers in the barcode are input correctly. So how can you make a check digit? First, add the 1st, 3rd, 5th, 7th, 9th, and 11th digits. Take the sum and multiply it by 3. Then, add the 2nd, 4th, 6th, 8th, and 10th digits. Add the first total to that total. After that, do a couple more mathematical operations and finally get the check digit.

New Words

barcode	universal
n a special code made of lines	*adj* used everywhere in the world

product	input
n something that is bought and sold	*v* put a number into a machine

add	multiply
v	*v*
ex Add 1 and 1. The total is 2.	**ex** Multiply 2 by 3. The total is 6.

Part A. Sentence Completion

1. A: What do the numbers under this barcode mean?
   B: Each number _____ special uses.

   (A) do
   (B) has
   (C) can
   (D) have

2. A: Why did you buy six water bottles? It's the two of us.
   B: We usually drink three each. So I multiplied 2 _____ 3.

   (A) by
   (B) on
   (C) for
   (D) with

Part B. Situational Writing

3.

   He uses a _____ at work.

   (A) diving mask
   (B) mobile phone
   (C) digital camera
   (D) barcode scanner

4.

   You need to _____ those two numbers to get 9.

   (A) add
   (B) divide
   (C) multiply
   (D) subtract

5. What do QR codes have that UPC barcodes do not have?

(A) fewer digits
(B) color variety
(C) self-correction
(D) laser capability

6. Which type of code can store "19A9BQ45839"?

(A) a UPC barcode
(B) a QR code
(C) both
(D) neither

Part D. General Reading and Retelling

In a supermarket, you can see many black and white barcodes. The barcodes connect to something called a "Universal Product Code." The first number in the code says what kind of product it is. For example, a "3" means that it is a beauty product. The 2nd to 6th digits show information about the product maker. The 7th to 11th numbers are about the store. And very importantly, each bar code has a "check digit." It is the 12th number in a bar code. The check digit is to see that the other numbers in the barcode are input correctly. So how can you make a check digit? First, add the 1st, 3rd, 5th, 7th, 9th, and 11th digits. Take the sum and multiply it by 3. Then, add the 2nd, 4th, 6th, 8th, and 10th digits. Add the first total to that total. After that, do a couple more mathematical operations and finally get the check digit.

7. Which of the following is the best title for the passage?

    (A) The Six Numbers in a Barcode
    (B) Why Barcodes Are No Longer Popular
    (C) How to Save Money at the Supermarket
    (D) The Numbers in Universal Product Codes

8. According to the passage, what does the first code number show?

    (A) type of product
    (B) color of product
    (C) when a product is sold
    (D) where a product is made

9. Which digits are about the store?

    (A) first and second
    (B) second to sixth
    (C) seventh to eleventh
    (D) twelfth and over

10. What is true about the check digit?

    (A) It is always the number 10.
    (B) It is the first digit in the code.
    (C) It shows that inputting is correct.
    (D) It proves that the product is new.

Listening Practice

 Listen and write.

  MP3 J1-8

Barcodes

In a supermarket, you can see many black and white ⁱ _____ . The barcodes connect to something called a " ² _____ Product Code." The first number in the code says what kind of product it is. For example, a "3" means that it is a beauty product. The 2ⁿᵈ to 6ᵗʰ digits show information about the ³ _____ maker. The 7ᵗʰ to 11ᵗʰ numbers are about the store. And very importantly, each bar code has a "check digit." It is the 12ᵗʰ number in a bar code. The check digit is to see that the other numbers in the barcode are ⁴ _____ correctly. So how can you make a check digit? First, ⁵ _____ the 1ˢᵗ, 3ʳᵈ, 5ᵗʰ, 7ᵗʰ, 9ᵗʰ, and 11ᵗʰ digits. Take the sum and ⁶ _____ it by 3. Then, add the 2ⁿᵈ, 4ᵗʰ, 6ᵗʰ, 8ᵗʰ, and 10ᵗʰ digits. Add the first total to that total. After that, do a couple more mathematical operations and finally get the check digit.

Word Bank

produt	barcodes	barcods
Universil	product	input
Universal	add	multiplies
multiply	added	inpet

 Listen. Pause. Say each sentence.

  MP3 J1-8G

Writing Practice

 Write the words.

1 _____

n   a special code made of lines

2 _____

adj   used everywhere in the world

3 _____

n   something that is bought and sold

4 _____

v   put a number into a machine

5 _____

v

ex   _____ 1 and 1. The total is 2.

6 _____

v

ex   _____ 2 by 3. The total is 6.

 Write the words in each blank.

Summary

Barcodes connect to a "Universal _____ Code." The first number says the type of product, the 2nd to 6th digits are about the product maker, and the _____ to 11th numbers are about the store. The 12th number is a "_____ digit." You can get the check digit by doing some _____ operations.

Word Puzzle

 Complete the word puzzle.

1↓ something that is bought and sold

2↓ _____ 1 and 1. The total is 2.

4↓ _____ 2 by 3. The total is 6.

3→ a special code made of lines

5→ used everywhere in the world

6→ put a number into a machine

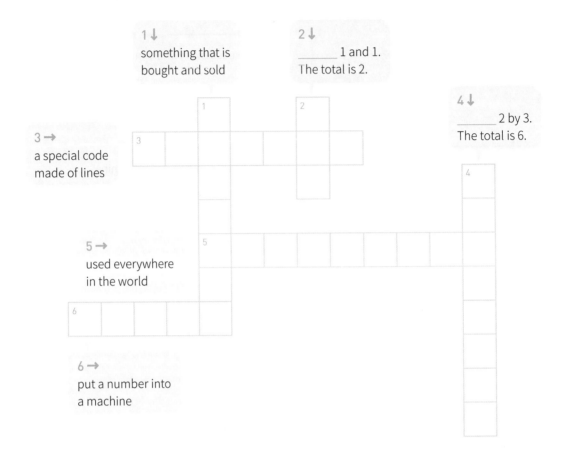

A Math Genius

Teacher's Book p.80

People often write to professors with crazy theories and ideas. In 1913, G.E. Hardy, an English mathematics professor, received ten pages from a stranger in India. The pages contained 120 mysterious math statements and formulas. At first Hardy probably thought the formulas meant nothing. But then he looked more closely. The formulas and statements were real. He thought they might be from a genius. That genius was Srinivasa Ramanujan.

Ramanujan loved math. However, his path to life as a mathematician was not easy. As a teenager, he did well in school. But when he was 16, he started studying for a very difficult math test. As he was studying, he became obsessed with the formulas in his exam preparation book. He used the formulas in the book to figure out new discoveries in math. He became so interested in math that he started to ignore all his other academic subjects. He failed his university exams many times. Eventually, he dropped out of university. He worked as a clerk until he wrote to Hardy.

Hardy wrote a reply to Ramanujan and they started to work together. Ramanujan's way of thinking about math was a mystery to Hardy and others. Ramanujan said that some of his ideas came to him while he was dreaming. By the time he died at the early age of 32, he had produced about 3,000 mathematical theories, formulas, and statements.

CHAPTER 3

Science

UNIT 9

The Water Cycle

 Teacher's Book p.81

Using the picture, can you explain the water cycle?

The water cycle is essential for everything on our planet. How does it work? First, the sun's energy heats up the earth. The world's lakes, oceans, and even tiny puddles get warmer. At this point, some of the water turns into a gas called "vapor." This process is called "evaporation." Water also comes off of plant leaves. That process is called "transpiration." Water gas from evaporation and transpiration rises up into the air. When it gets high in the sky, it becomes colder and turns into clouds. This process is called "condensation." When there is too much condensation, water drops in the clouds become too heavy. At this point, the water falls to the earth in the form of rain or snow. This is called "precipitation." Some of the water goes back into the lakes, oceans, and puddles. This process is called "collection." Some more of the water goes into the ground. After some time, the water in the ground goes back to the lakes or oceans. And then the whole cycle starts again!

New Words

cycle *n* events that are repeated	**essential** *adj* necessary
puddle *n* a small patch of water on the ground	**vapor** *n* a form of gas
at this point *adv* then	**after some time** *adv* after a while

Part A. **Sentence Completion**

1.　A: What happens after water turns into a gas and rises up?

　　B: When it gets really _____ up in the sky, it turns into clouds.

　　(A)　high
　　(B)　highs
　　(C)　height
　　(D)　heighten

2.　A: Water moves into the air through a plant's leaves.

　　B: That's a process _____ "transpiration."

　　(A)　called
　　(B)　to call
　　(C)　calling
　　(D)　be called

Part B. **Situational Writing**

3.

You can see pink _____ coming out of the top of the lab equipment.

　　(A)　gum
　　(B)　vapor
　　(C)　plants
　　(D)　flowers

4.

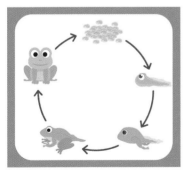

This chart shows the _____ of a frog.

　　(A)　life cycle
　　(B)　typical diet
　　(C)　hunting habits
　　(D)　common enemies

UNIT 9　The Water Cycle

Getting Fresh Water Using a Solar Still

It is not good to drink water from the ocean, but if you have a solar still, you can make water that is safe to drink!

1 Sunlight enters the solar still, but it cannot escape.

2 Water vapor cools on the dome of the solar still. When enough gathers, the heavy water drops run down the side of the dome.

3 The inside of the solar still heats up. The water becomes so hot that vapor floats to the top, but the ocean's salts stay at the bottom.

4 The fresh water goes into a container. After a while, there is enough clean water to drink!

5. What is true about a solar still?

(A) It cools down water.
(B) It blocks the sunlight.
(C) It turns salt into vapor.
(D) It is used to get safe water.

6. What material is the solar still's dome most likely made of?

(A) hard wood
(B) clear plastic
(C) frozen water
(D) brown leather

Part D. General Reading and Retelling

The water cycle is essential for everything on our planet. How does it work? First, the sun's energy heats up the earth. The world's lakes, oceans, and even tiny puddles get warmer. At this point, some of the water turns into a gas called "vapor." This process is called "evaporation." Water also comes off of plant leaves. That process is called "transpiration." Water gas from evaporation and transpiration rises up into the air. When it gets high in the sky, it becomes colder and turns into clouds. This process is called "condensation." When there is too much condensation, water drops in the clouds become too heavy. At this point, the water falls to the earth in the form of rain or snow. This is called "precipitation." Some of the water goes back into the lakes, oceans, and puddles. This process is called "collection." Some more of the water goes into the ground. After some time, the water in the ground goes back to the lakes or oceans. And then the whole cycle starts again!

7. What is the passage mainly about?

    (A) how water freezes
    (B) how the water cycle works
    (C) how people can save water
    (D) how to prevent water pollution

8. What can happen when there is too much condensation in a cloud?

    (A) It rains or snows.
    (B) The cloud evaporates.
    (C) Water rises from plants.
    (D) Puddles begin to disappear.

9. Which stage is NOT mentioned?

    (A) collection
    (B) pollination
    (C) precipitation
    (D) condensation

10. Which water collection place is mentioned?

    (A) dams
    (B) buckets
    (C) puddles
    (D) supermarkets

UNIT 9   The Water Cycle

Listening Practice

 Listen and write.

  MP3 J1-9

The Water Cycle

The water ¹ _____ is ² _____ for everything on our planet. How does it work? First, the sun's energy heats up the earth. The world's lakes, oceans, and even tiny ³ _____ get warmer. At this point, some of the water turns into a gas called " ⁴ _____ ." This process is called "evaporation." Water also comes off of plant leaves. That process is called "transpiration." Water gas from evaporation and transpiration rises up into the air. When it gets high in the sky, it becomes colder and turns into clouds. This process is called "condensation." When there is too much condensation, water drops in the clouds become too heavy. ⁵ _____ , the water falls to the earth in the form of rain or snow. This is called "precipitation." Some of the water goes back into the lakes, oceans, and puddles. This process is called "collection." Some more of the water goes into the ground. After ⁶ _____ , the water in the ground goes back to the lakes or oceans. And then the whole cycle starts again!

Word Bank

essential	At this point	essencial
vapor	sumtime	puddles
bapor	pudles	cycle
Athispoint	sickle	some time

 Listen. Pause. Say each sentence.

  MP3 J1-9G

Writing Practice

Write the words.

1 _____

n events that are repeated

2 _____

adj necessary

3 _____

n a small patch of water on the ground

4 _____

n a form of gas

5 _____

adv then

6 _____

adv after a while

Write the words in each blank.

Summary

The water _____ is _____. The sun's energy heats up the earth, and the water goes up into the air. This _____ into clouds. After a while, it becomes rain or snow and falls to the _____. Then the water goes back to the lakes or oceans. The whole cycle starts again!

Word Puzzle

 Complete the word puzzle.

1 → necessary

2 ↓ after a while

3 ↓ a form of gas

4 → events that are repeated

5 → then

6 → a small patch of water on the ground

UNIT 10

Teacher's Book
p.85

Earth Day

Do you celebrate Earth Day where you live?
What kind of things do you do?

April 22 is Earth Day. The first Earth Day was held in 1970 and began in the U.S. Twenty million people took part. They cleaned streets, made speeches, and even listened to poems about the earth. A lot of young people participated in the first Earth Day. In fact, the date of April 22 was chosen because it came between university students' holidays and their final exams. Many people thought the first Earth Day was silly. They wondered how protests, poems, and songs could help the Earth. However, it seems that Earth Day did change some people's opinions. In 1969, researchers asked Americans whether it was important to protect the environment. Fewer than 1% said it was. In 1971, the researchers asked people again. This time 25% of the public thought it was important to protect the environment. Today, Earth Day has become an international celebration. Around the world, it is known as "International Mother Earth Day." Each year, around a billion people participate in events for that day.

New Words

speech *n* a talk	**participate in** *v* take part in
be chosen *v* be selected	**silly** *adj* not serious
environment *n* nature	**celebration** *n* a happy event

Part A. Sentence Completion

1. A: Next Monday is Earth Day.
    B: Yes! It is important _____ our planet.

    (A) protect
    (B) to protect
    (C) protected
    (D) protecting

2. A: So many people attended your Earth Day concert!
    B: I had thought there would only be a few, _____ thousands of people came!

    (A) or
    (B) so
    (C) for
    (D) but

Part B. Situational Writing

3.

He is _____ about climate change.

(A) giving a speech
(B) making a poster
(C) showing a movie
(D) listening to a lecture

4.

I planted some herbs in a _____ for Earth Day.

(A) pot
(B) tank
(C) field
(D) glass

We all know that trees and other plants are important for turning carbon dioxide (CO_2) into oxygen. But what kinds of trees do the job better than all the others? Here are some basic rules for finding oxygen super-producers!

1. Leafy green!

Trees make oxygen in their leaves. So, the more leaves (or needles) the trees have, the more they can produce!

2. How much wood?

Trees with lots of woody parts like trunks and branches need more CO_2 to grow, so they'll make more oxygen, too.

3. Bigger is better!

As a general rule, big trees pump out more oxygen faster.

4. Time and place

Even a big tree cannot produce maximum oxygen in the wrong weather or soil conditions. Trees need the correct environment to grow and produce oxygen.

5. Which of the following would most likely produce more oxygen than others?

(A) a tall tree with few leaves

(B) a tall tree with many leaves

(C) a short tree with few leaves

(D) a short tree with many leaves

6. Which person would find this passage LEAST helpful to do their job?

(A) a gardener

(B) a forest ranger

(C) a biology researcher

(D) a construction worker

Part D. General Reading and Retelling

April 22 is Earth Day. The first Earth Day was held in 1970 and began in the U.S. Twenty million people took part. They cleaned streets, made speeches, and even listened to poems about the earth. A lot of young people participated in the first Earth Day. In fact, the date of April 22 was chosen because it came between university students' holidays and their final exams. Many people thought the first Earth Day was silly. They wondered how protests, poems, and songs could help the Earth. However, it seems that Earth Day did change some people's opinions. In 1969, researchers asked Americans whether it was important to protect the environment. Fewer than 1% said it was. In 1971, the researchers asked people again. This time 25% of the public thought it was important to protect the environment. Today, Earth Day has become an international celebration. Around the world, it is known as "International Mother Earth Day." Each year, around a billion people participate in events for that day.

7. According to the passage, what is true about Earth Day?

(A) It is on April 22nd.
(B) It began in England.
(C) It happens in summer.
(D) It started in the 1980s.

8. According to the passage, why was Earth Day's date chosen?

(A) so that taxi drivers could join
(B) so that parents could see kids perform
(C) so that people could see protests on TV
(D) so that university students could participate

9. According to the passage, which of the following did people most likely do at the first Earth Day event?

(A) run a marathon
(B) unplug their electrical devices
(C) read out poems about the planet
(D) donate money to children's hospitals

10. Around how many people participate in Earth Day events each year now?

(A) 100,000
(B) 1,000,000
(C) 10,000,000
(D) 1,000,000,000

Listening Practice

 Listen and write.

  MP3 J1-10

Earth Day

April 22 is Earth Day. The first Earth Day was held in 1970 and began in the U.S.
Twenty million people took part. They cleaned streets, made [1] _____, and
even listened to poems about the earth. A lot of young people [2] _____ in
the first Earth Day. In fact, the date of April 22 was [3] _____ because it
came between university students' holidays and their final exams. Many people thought
the first Earth Day was [4] _____. They wondered how protests, poems, and
songs could help the Earth. However, it seems that Earth Day did change some people's
opinions. In 1969, researchers asked Americans whether it was important to protect the
environment. Fewer than 1% said it was. In 1971, the researchers asked people again.
This time 25% of the public thought it was important to protect [5] _____ .
Today, Earth Day has become an international [6] _____ . Around the world,
it is known as "International Mother Earth Day." Each year, around a billion people
participate in events for that day.

Word Bank

participaded	speeches	environment
speech	chosen	choosen
celebrasion	the environment	sillie
silly	celebration	participated

 Listen. Pause. Say each sentence.

  MP3 J1-10G

Writing Practice

Write the words.

1 _____

n a talk

2 _____

v take part in

3 _____

v be selected

4 _____

adj not serious

5 _____

n nature

6 _____

n a happy event

 Write the words in each blank.

Summary

April _____ is Earth Day. Many people thought the first Earth Day was

_____. However, as time went by, it changed some people's opinions. Earth

Day has now become an international _____. Each year, around a

_____ people participate in events for that day.

Word Puzzle

 Complete the word puzzle.

1↓ not serious

2↓ nature

3↓ a happy event

1→ a talk

4→ be selected

5→ take part in

UNIT 11

Lightning

Teacher's Book p.90

When is the last time you saw lightning?
How hot do you think the lightning bolt was?

Did you know that lightning flashes more than 3 million times every day around the world? That is just one of the reasons why lightning is so awesome. Here are some other cool facts about lightning. First, lightning is incredibly fast. After the first flash, it can travel at up to half the speed of light. If lightning went to the moon, it would only take a few seconds. Second, even though each lightning bolt is really long (1.6 - 3.2 km), each lightning bolt is very narrow. You may be shocked to learn that a lightning bolt is just 2 to 3 centimeters wide! But even though it is not wide, a lightning bolt is still very hot. The temperature can reach up to 30,000°C. That is five times hotter than the sun's surface. Finally, humans can cause lightning to happen. More specifically, helicopters can make an electrical current. The current can trigger lightning. In conclusion, lightning may be hot, but facts about lightning are really cool.

New Words

lightning	**flash**
n electricity in the sky	*n* a sudden bright light
lightning bolt	**electrical current**
n lightning that looks like a white line	*n* a wave of electricity
helicopter 	**trigger**
n a machine that flies by lifting up directly	*v* make an event start

Part A. Sentence Completion

1. A: I was almost struck by lightning.
    B: Do you know lightning can be _____ than the sun?

    (A) five times hotter
    (B) five hotter times
    (C) hotter times five
    (D) hotter five times

2. A: _____ would it take for lightning to reach the moon?
    B: Probably four or five seconds. It is very fast.

    (A) What day
    (B) How long
    (C) What time
    (D) How many

Part B. Situational Writing

3.

    The lights on top of the police car are _____.

    (A) flashing
    (B) stopped
    (C) turned off
    (D) black and white

4.

    It's a lightning _____.

    (A) bug
    (B) bolt
    (C) bird
    (D) bass

The Venezuela Times

March, 2010

The famous Catatumbo lightning has still not returned. Since January of this year, the intense nightly lightning storms in this part of Venezuela have not occurred. In most years, the area where the Catatumbo River meets Lake Maracaibo had over 40,000 bolts of lightning a night for up to 300 nights a year, but now the skies are dark. What can account for this change? Scientists believe that drought may be responsible. Others think it is a result of changing air and ocean temperatures. In any case, it is hoped that the world-famous lightning will come back soon.

5. What problem does the article mention?

    (A) fewer fish in a lake
    (B) year of too much rain
    (C) months of no lightning
    (D) reduced tourist numbers

6. Which of the following about typical Catatumbo lightning is NOT true?

    (A) It may be caused by drought.
    (B) It occurs where a lake meets a river.
    (C) Each night has 40,000 bolts of lightning.
    (D) It typically occurs up to 300 nights a year.

Did you know that lightning flashes more than 3 million times every day around the world? That is just one of the reasons why lightning is so awesome. Here are some other cool facts about lightning. First, lightning is incredibly fast. After the first flash, it can travel at up to half the speed of light. If lightning went to the moon, it would only take a few seconds. Second, even though each lightning bolt is really long (1.6 - 3.2 km), each lightning bolt is very narrow. You may be shocked to learn that a lightning bolt is just 2 to 3 centimeters wide! But even though it is not wide, a lightning bolt is still very hot. The temperature can reach up to 30,000°C. That is five times hotter than the sun's surface. Finally, humans can cause lightning to happen. More specifically, helicopters can make an electrical current. The current can trigger lightning. In conclusion, lightning may be hot, but facts about lightning are really cool.

7. What is the best title for this passage?

   (A) Why Lightning is Fast
   (B) What Triggers Lightning
   (C) Interesting Facts about Lightning
   (D) The Difference between Lightning and Thunder

8. Which of the following is mentioned about lightning?

   (A) It can help plants grow.
   (B) A Venezuelan lake is most hit.
   (C) It flashes over 3 million times each day.
   (D) It can turn beach sand into a kind of glass.

9. What is true about lightning bolts?

   (A) They look wider than their length.
   (B) They are almost as wide as they are long.
   (C) They are over 1.6 km long and up to 3 centimeters wide.
   (D) They are under 3.2 km long and over 3 centimeters wide.

10. According to the passage, what can trigger lightning?

   (A) kites
   (B) mirrors
   (C) lightbulbs
   (D) helicopters

UNIT 11　Lightning

Listen and write.

  MP3 J1-11

Lightning

Did you know that lightning flashes more than 3 million times every day around the world? That is just one of the reasons why ¹_____ is so awesome. Here are some other cool facts about lightning. First, lightning is incredibly fast. After the first ²_____, it can travel at up to half the speed of light. If lightning went to the moon, it would only take a few seconds. Second, even though each lightning ³_____ is really long (1.6 - 3.2 km), each lightning bolt is very narrow. You may be shocked to learn that a lightning bolt is just 2 to 3 centimeters wide! But even though it is not wide, a lightning bolt is still very hot. The temperature can reach up to 30,000°C. That is five times hotter than the sun's surface. Finally, humans can cause lightning to happen. More specifically, ⁴_____ can make an ⁵_____ current. The current can ⁶_____ lightning. In conclusion, lightning may be hot, but facts about lightning are really cool.

Word Bank

bolt	flash	electricle
volt	trigger	electrical
helgicopters	lightning	lightnings
plash	helicopters	triger

 Listen. Pause. Say each sentence.

  MP3 J1-11G

Writing Practice

 Write the words.

1 _____

n electricity in the sky

2 _____

n a sudden bright light

3 _____

n lightning that looks like a white line

4 _____

n a wave of electricity

5 _____

n a machine that flies by lifting up directly

6 _____

v make an event start

 Write the words in each blank.

Summary

_____ is awesome for many reasons. It _____ more than

3 _____ times every day, and it is incredibly fast. Although it is very

_____, each lightning bolt is very hot. Also, humans can cause lightning to

happen. In short, lightning is really interesting.

Word Puzzle

  Complete the word puzzle.

1 → electricity in the sky

2 ↓ make an event start

3 ↓ a wave of electricity

4 → a sudden bright light

6 → a machine that flies by lifting up directly

5 ↓ lightning that looks like a white line

UNIT 12

Superbugs

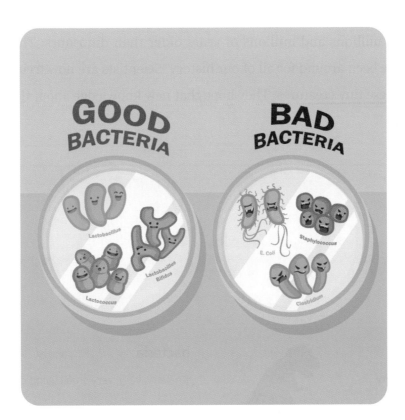

Are superbugs good bacteria or bad bacteria?
What might they do?

UNIT 12 Superbugs

They have been on the earth longer than the dinosaurs. And they are much scarier than a T-Rex. What are they? They are superbugs. Superbugs are bacteria. There are many types of bacteria on the earth. Some of them are very helpful to humans. Some live in our bodies and help us digest food. Those are good bacteria. Superbugs, however, are really bad. They cannot be treated with the medicine we have. Scientists used to think that superbugs were from modern times. They thought that humans made superbugs through modern medicine. Now they think that superbugs are really old. In fact, superbugs are millions and millions of years older than dinosaurs. That means that superbugs have been around for all of our history. Scientists are now trying to find ways to eliminate these tiny creatures. They hope that new knowledge about these superbugs will help.

New Words

dinosaur

n a reptile from a very, very long time ago

bacteria

n very, very, very small living creatures

superbug

n a bad type of bacteria

digest

v break down (food)

in fact

adv actually

eliminate X

v make X go away

Part A. Sentence Completion

1. A: The weather report says it will rain today.
   B: Yes, I know. _____, I can see rain clouds already.

   (A) While
   (B) In fact
   (C) Despite
   (D) In spite of

2. A: Why do you keep washing your hands?
   B: It is important to _____ infections.

   (A) avoid
   (B) avoids
   (C) avoided
   (D) avoiding

Part B. Situational Writing

3.

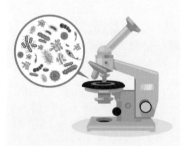

Let's look at the _____ in the laboratory.

(A) sheep
(B) rabbits
(C) bacteria
(D) computers

4.

The dog thinks, "This cat is _____."

(A) scary
(B) sweet
(C) scared
(D) sleeping

How to Avoid Superbugs

| STEP 01 | Use soap and water to wash your hands. |

| STEP 02 | Avoid sharing towels with other people. |

| STEP 03 | Get the vaccinations recommended by your doctor. Being sick with the flu or other illnesses can be risky when it comes to superbug infections. |

| STEP 04 | Do not use antibiotics if you have a virus. They will not help, and they can cause superbugs. |

| STEP 05 | Sometimes farmers inject animals with antibiotics. Eating organic meat can help avoid the spread of superbugs from antibiotics. |

5. What does the passage say about towels?

   (A) You should use large ones.
   (B) You should not share them.
   (C) You should not use white ones.
   (D) You should wash them in hot water.

6. Which of the following is NOT a recommended step?

   (A) getting vaccinations
   (B) eating organic meat
   (C) using antibiotics to treat a virus
   (D) washing hands in soap and water

Part D. General Reading and Retelling

They have been on the earth longer than the dinosaurs. And they are much scarier than a T-Rex. What are they? They are superbugs. Superbugs are bacteria. There are many types of bacteria on the earth. Some of them are very helpful to humans. Some live in our bodies and help us digest food. Those are good bacteria. Superbugs, however, are really bad. They cannot be treated with the medicine we have. Scientists used to think that superbugs were from modern times. They thought that humans made superbugs through modern medicine. Now they think that superbugs are really old. In fact, superbugs are millions and millions of years older than dinosaurs. That means that superbugs have been around for all of our history. Scientists are now trying to find ways to eliminate these tiny creatures. They hope that new knowledge about these superbugs will help.

7. What is the passage mainly about?

    (A) medicine
    (B) dinosaurs
    (C) superbugs
    (D) researchers

8. What does the writer claim about superbugs?

    (A) They are from modern times.
    (B) They are scarier than a T-Rex.
    (C) They are a good type of bacteria.
    (D) They are only helpful to humans.

9. What is mentioned about superbugs?

    (A) They existed before humans.
    (B) They spread fast in hospitals.
    (C) They adapt quickly to new bodies.
    (D) They jumped between humans and animals.

10. What would a scientist most likely say about superbugs?

    (A) "These are so easy to stop!"
    (B) "You should eat them daily."
    (C) "We need to protect ourselves from them."
    (D) "I made these superbugs from dinosaur bones."

Listen and write.

  MP3 J1-12

Superbugs

They have been on the earth longer than the ¹ _____ . And they are much scarier than a T-Rex. What are they? They are ² _____ . Superbugs are ³ _____ . There are many types of bacteria on the earth. Some of them are very helpful to humans. Some live in our bodies and help us ⁴ _____ food. Those are good bacteria. Superbugs, however, are really bad. They cannot be treated with the medicine we have. Scientists used to think that superbugs were from modern times. They thought that humans made superbugs through modern medicine. Now they think that superbugs are really old. ⁵ _____ , superbugs are millions and millions of years older than dinosaurs. That means that superbugs have been around for all of our history. Scientists are now trying to find ways to ⁶ _____ these tiny creatures. They hope that new knowledge about these superbugs will help.

Word Bank

eliminete	Infact	dinosaurs
superbug	dinosaur	In fact
eliminate	superbugs	digest
dijest	becteria	bacteria

 Listen. Pause. Say each sentence.

  MP3 J1-12G

Writing Practice

 Write the words.

1 _____

   n a reptile from a very, very long time ago

2 _____

   n very, very, very small living creatures

3 _____

   n a bad type of bacteria

4 _____

   v break down (food)

5 _____

   adv actually

6 _____ **X**

   v make X go away

 Write the words in each blank.

Summary

Superbugs are bacteria. Some bacteria are very _____ to humans.

But _____ are really bad, and they have been around for all of our history.

They cannot be treated with _____ we have. Scientists are now trying to find

ways to _____ these tiny creatures.

Word Puzzle

 Complete the word puzzle.

1 ↓
a reptile from a very,
very long time ago

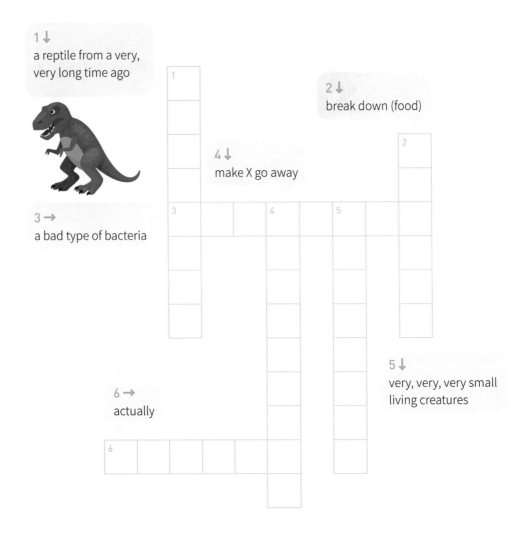

2 ↓
break down (food)

4 ↓
make X go away

3 →
a bad type of bacteria

5 ↓
very, very, very small
living creatures

6 →
actually

The Strange Light of Gurdon

Teacher's Book p.100

If you go to the small town of Gurdon, Arkansas, in the US, you may find yourself looking at a strange light in the trees. It is near the railroad tracks, but it is not a train. It is not from a car; there is no road in the forest. And yet, the light moves. Sometimes the light is blue-white. Sometimes the light is orange. Is it, as legend claims, the ghost of a railroad worker carrying a lantern?

Some scientists believe the light comes from an effect called "piezoelectricity." When certain materials are bent or squeezed, an electric reaction can occur. The town of Gurdon is near a mine. In the mine are crystals. It is possible that the electric reaction from the squeezed materials combines with something from the crystals. Perhaps that causes the light. Scientists say that the light is always there, but you can only see it at night.

Go to the trees near the highway in Gurdon and see the light for yourself. But be careful when you do. If you hear the sound of a railroad worker looking for his lantern, run!

ANSWERS

CHAPTER 1 | Neighbors p.10

UNIT 1 · J1-1 · p.11

	1	2	3	4	5	6	7	8	9	10
⏱	1 (C)	2 (B)	3 (B)	4 (A)	5 (D)	6 (D)	7 (D)	8 (B)	9 (D)	10 (A)
🎧	1 sign language	2 researcher	3 certain	4 According to	5 allowed	6 looked like				
✏	1 sign language	2 researcher	3 certain	4 according to	5 be allowed to	6 look like				

📄 different, gorilla, sign language, humans

※ → 1 according to 6 look like ↓ 2 certain 3 sign language 4 be allowed to 5 researcher

UNIT 2 · J1-2 · p.19

	1	2	3	4	5	6	7	8	9	10
⏱	1 (A)	2 (D)	3 (C)	4 (A)	5 (C)	6 (D)	7 (B)	8 (C)	9 (D)	10 (D)
🎧	1 earthquakes	2 chemicals	3 ponds	4 behavior	5 connected	6 perhaps				
✏	1 earthquake	2 chemical	3 pond	4 behavior	5 be connected to	6 perhaps				

📄 earthquakes, act, wonder, behaviors

※ → 1 pond 3 behavior 5 chemical ↓ 1 perhaps 2 be connected to 4 earthquake

UNIT 3 · J1-3 · p.27

	1	2	3	4	5	6	7	8	9	10
⏱	1 (B)	2 (D)	3 (C)	4 (C)	5 (D)	6 (C)	7 (D)	8 (C)	9 (B)	10 (C)
🎧	1 incredible	2 incredibly	3 flexible	4 hold their breath	5 swallow	6 lungs				
✏	1 incredible	2 incredibly	3 flexible	4 swallow	5 hold your breath	6 lungs				

📄 incredible, flexible, breath, superpowers

※ → 2 lungs 5 incredible ↓ 1 hold your breath 3 flexible 4 swallow 6 incredibly

UNIT 4 · J1-4 · p.35

	1	2	3	4	5	6	7	8	9	10
⏱	1 (B)	2 (C)	3 (B)	4 (D)	5 (B)	6 (D)	7 (C)	8 (C)	9 (D)	10 (D)
🎧	1 pigeons	2 residents	3 Tame	4 key to	5 crucial	6 In short				
✏	1 pigeon	2 resident	3 tame	4 key to	5 crucial	6 in short				

📄 hate, history, wars, In short

※ → 2 crucial 4 resident 6 key to ↓ 1 pigeon 3 in short 5 tame

CHAPTER 2 | Neighborhood p.44

UNIT 5 · J1-5 · p.45

	1	2	3	4	5	6	7	8	9	10
⏱	1 (A)	2 (B)	3 (C)	4 (A)	5 (A)	6 (A)	7 (D)	8 (C)	9 (A)	10 (D)
🎧	1 Athletes	2 mathematician	3 medal	4 ancient	5 criticize	6 honor				
✏	1 athlete	2 medal	3 mathematician	4 ancient	5 criticize	6 big honor				

📄 mathematicians, research, 40, honor

※ → 1 medal 5 big honor ↓ 1 mathematician 2 athlete 3 ancient 4 criticize

UNIT 6 · J1-6 · p.53

	1	2	3	4	5	6	7	8	9	10
⏱	1 (D)	2 (A)	3 (A)	4 (D)	5 (D)	6 (D)	7 (C)	8 (C)	9 (B)	10 (A)
🎧	1 statistics	2 predictions	3 diseases	4 cancer	5 strategies	6 make sure				
✏	1 statistic	2 make predictions	3 disease	4 cancer	5 strategy	6 make sure				

📄 statistics, weather, diseases, sports, useful

※ → 5 strategy 6 statistic ↓ 1 cancer 2 make sure 3 disease 4 make predictions

UNIT 7 · J1-7 · p.61

	1	2	3	4	5	6	7	8	9	10
⏱	1 (C)	2 (B)	3 (B)	4 (A)	5 (D)	6 (B)	7 (C)	8 (C)	9 (B)	10 (C)
🎧	1 equals	2 approximately	3 ratio	4 spirals	5 hurricanes	6 Calculating				
✏	1 ratio	2 equal	3 approximately	4 hurricane	5 spiral	6 calculate				

📄 Ratio, nature, number, world

※ → 1 spiral 5 calculate ↓ 2 approximately 3 hurricane 4 ratio 6 equal

UNIT 8 · J1-8 · p.69

	1	2	3	4	5	6	7	8	9	10
⏱	1 (B)	2 (A)	3 (D)	4 (A)	5 (C)	6 (B)	7 (D)	8 (A)	9 (C)	10 (C)
🎧	1 barcodes	2 Universal	3 product	4 input	5 add	6 multiply				
✏	1 barcode	2 universal	3 product	4 input	5 add	6 multiply				

📄 Product, 7th, check, mathematical

※ → 3 barcode 5 universal 6 input ↓ 1 product 2 add 4 multiply

CHAPTER 3 | Stadium in My Town p.78

UNIT 9 · J1-9 · p.79

	1	2	3	4	5	6	7	8	9	10
⏱	1 (A)	2 (A)	3 (B)	4 (A)	5 (D)	6 (B)	7 (B)	8 (A)	9 (B)	10 (C)
🎧	1 cycle	2 essential	3 puddles	4 vapor	5 At this point	6 some time				
✏	1 cycle	2 essential	3 puddle	4 vapor	5 at this point	6 after some time				

📄 cycle, essential, condenses, ground

※ → 1 essential 4 cycle 5 at this point 6 puddle ↓ 2 after some time 3 vapor

UNIT 10 · J1-10 · p.87

	1	2	3	4	5	6	7	8	9	10
⏱	1 (B)	2 (D)	3 (A)	4 (A)	5 (D)	6 (D)	7 (A)	8 (D)	9 (C)	10 (D)
🎧	1 speeches	2 participated	3 chosen	4 silly	5 the environment	6 celebration				
✏	1 speech	2 participate in	3 be chosen	4 silly	5 environment	6 celebration				

📄 22, silly, celebration, billion

※ → 1 speech 4 be chosen 5 participate in ↓ 1 silly 2 environment 3 celebration

UNIT 11 · J1-11 · p.95

	1	2	3	4	5	6	7	8	9	10
⏱	1 (A)	2 (B)	3 (A)	4 (B)	5 (C)	6 (A)	7 (C)	8 (C)	9 (C)	10 (D)
🎧	1 lightning	2 flash	3 bolt	4 helicopters	5 electrical	6 trigger				
✏	1 lightning	2 flash	3 lightning bolt	4 electrical current	5 helicopter	6 trigger				

📄 Lightning, flashes, million, narrow

※ → 1 lightning 4 flash 6 helicopter ↓ 2 trigger 3 electrical current 5 lightning bolt

UNIT 12 · J1-12 · p.103

	1	2	3	4	5	6	7	8	9	10
⏱	1 (B)	2 (A)	3 (C)	4 (A)	5 (D)	6 (C)	7 (C)	8 (B)	9 (A)	10 (C)
🎧	1 dinosaurs	2 superbugs	3 bacteria	4 digest	5 In fact	6 eliminate				
✏	1 dinosaur	2 bacteria	3 superbug	4 digest	5 in fact	6 eliminate				

📄 helpful, superbugs, medicines, eliminate

※ → 3 superbug 6 in fact ↓ 1 dinosaur 2 digest 4 eliminate 5 bacteria

AI 빅데이터 기반 영어성장 플랫폼

TOSEL® Lab

공동기획
- 고려대학교 문과대학 언어정보연구소
- 고려대학교 공과대학 기계학습 및 빅 데이터연구원
- 국제토셀위원회

TOSEL Lab이란?

엄선된 100만 명의 응시자 성적 데이터를 활용한
AI기반 데이터 공유 및 가치 고도화 플랫폼

국내외 15,000여 개 학교·학원 단체응시인원 중 엄선한 100만 명 이상의 실제 TOSEL 성적 데이터와,
정부(과학기술정보통신부)의 연구지원으로 개발된 **맞춤식 AI 빅데이터 기반 영어성장 플랫폼**입니다.

TOSEL Lab Brand Identity

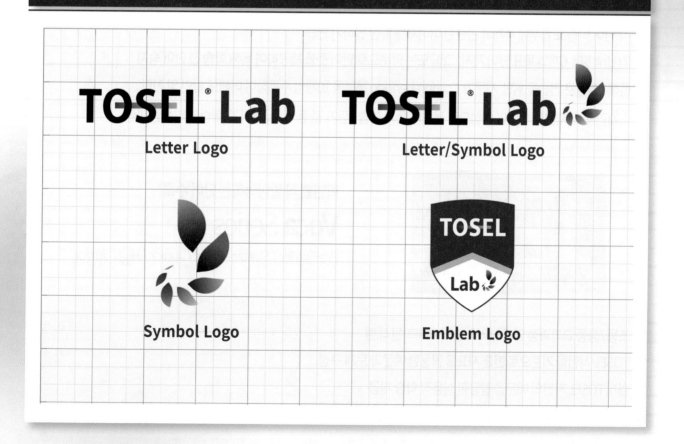

Letter Logo

Letter/Symbol Logo

Symbol Logo

Emblem Logo

TOSEL Lab에는 어떤 콘텐츠가 있나요?

진단

맞춤형 레벨테스트로
정확한 평가 제공

Placement Test

응시자 빅데이터 분석에
기반한 테스트로 신규 상담
학생의 영어능력을 정확하게
진단하고 효과적인 영어 교육
을 실시하기 위한 객관적인
가이드라인을 제공합니다.

교재

세분화된 레벨로
실력에 맞는 학습 제공

Book Content

TOSEL의 세분화된 교재 레벨
은 각 연령에 맞는 어휘와 읽기
지능 및 교과 과정과의 연계가
가능하도록 설계된 교재들로
효과적인 학습 커리큘럼을
제공합니다.

자기주도학습

교재와 연계한 다양한 콘텐츠로
효과적인 학습 제공

Study Content

Monthly Test를 대비한
다양한 콘텐츠를 제공해 영어
학습에 시너지 효과를 기대할
수 있으며, 학생들의 자기주도
학습 습관을 더 탄탄하게 키울
수 있습니다.

내신과 **토셀 고득점**을 한꺼번에!

Reading Series

Pre-Starter / Starter / Basic / Junior / High Junior

- 각 단어 학습 도입부에 주제와 관련된 이미지를 통한 말하기 연습
- 각 Unit별 4-6개의 목표 단어 제시, 그림 또는 영문으로 단어 뜻을 제공하여 독해 학습 전 단어 숙지
- 독해&실용문 연습을 위한 지문과 Comprehension 문항을 10개씩 수록하여 이해도 확인 및 진단
- 숙지한 독해 지문을 원어민 음성으로 들으며 듣기 학습, 듣기 전, 듣기 중, 듣기 후 학습 커리큘럼 마련

학년별 꼭 알아야하는 **단어 수록!**

Voca Series

Pre-Starter / Starter / Basic / Junior / High Junior

- 초등 / 중등 교과과정 연계 단어 학습과 세분화된 레벨
- TOSEL 시험을 기준으로 빈출 지표를 활용한 예문과 문제 구성
- 실제 TOSEL 지문의 예문을 활용한 실용적 학습 제공
- 실전 감각 향상과 점검을 위한 실전 문제 수록

체계적인 단계별 **문법 지침서**
Grammar Series
Pre-Starter / Starter / Basic / Junior / High Junior

- 초등 / 중등 교과과정 연계 문법 학습과 세분화된 레벨
- TOSEL 기출 문제 연습과 최신 수능 출제 문법을 포함하여 수능 / 내신 대비 가능
- 이해하기 쉬운 그림, 깔끔하게 정리된 표와 설명, 다양한 문제를 통해 문법 학습
- 실전 감각 향상과 점검을 위한 기출 문제 수록

한국 **학생들에게** 최적화된 듣기 실력 완성!
Listening Series
Pre-Starter / Starter / Basic / Junior / High Junior

- 초등 / 중등 교과과정 연계 말하기&듣기 학습과 세분화된 레벨
- TOSEL 기출 문장과 실생활에 자주 활용되는 문장 패턴을 통해 듣기 및 말하기 학습
- 실제 TOSEL 지문의 예문을 활용한 실용적 학습 제공
- 실전 감각 향상과 점검을 위한 기출 문제 수록

재미와 실력이 **동시에!**
Story Series
Pre-Starter / Starter / Basic / Junior

- 초등 / 중등 교과과정 연계 영어 학습과 세분화된 레벨
- 이야기 지문과 단어를 함께 연결지어 학생들의 독해 능력을 평가
- 이해하기 쉬운 그림, 깔끔하게 정리된 표와 설명, 다양한 문제, 재미있는 스토리를 통한 독해 학습
- 다양한 단계의 문항을 풀어보고 학생들의 읽기, 듣기, 쓰기, 말하기 실력을 집중적으로 향상

교재를 100% 활용하는 TOSEL Lab 지정교육기관의 노하우!

Teaching Materials

TOSEL에서 제공하는 수업 자료로
교재 학습을 더욱 효과적으로 진행!

Study Content

철저한 자기주도학습 콘텐츠로
교재 수업 후 효과적인 복습!

Test Content

교재 학습과 더불어 학생 맞춤형
시험으로 실력 점검 및 향상

Book Content

100만 명으로 엄선된 TOSEL
성적 데이터로 탄생!

국제토셀위원회는 TOSEL Lab 지정교육기관에서 교재로
수업하는 학원을 위해 교재를 잘 활용할 수 있는 다양한
콘텐츠를 제공 및 지원합니다.

**TOSEL Lab 지정교육기관을 위한 콘텐츠로
더욱 효과적인 수업을 경험하세요.**

TOSEL Lab 지정교육기관은

국제토셀위원회 직속 TOSEL연구소에서 20년 동안 보유해온 전국 15,000여 개
교육기관 토셀 응시자들의 영어성적 분석데이터를 공유받아, 통계를 기반으로 한
전문적이고 과학적인 커리큘럼을 설계하고, 영어학습 방향을 제시하여, 경쟁력있는
기관, 잘 가르치는 기관으로 해당 지역에서 입지를 다지게 됩니다.

**TOSEL Lab 지정교육기관으로 선정되기 위해서는
소정의 심사 절차가 수반됩니다.**

TOSEL Lab
더 알아보기

Tel. 02-953-0202
www.lab.tosel.co.kr

TOSEL Lab
심사신청하기